A GIFT FOR

_____

FROM

_____

Dr. Henry Cloud
& Dr. John Townsend

What to Do When You Don't Know What to Do

Bad Habits & Addictions

God Will Make a Way

INTEGRITY
PUBLISHERS

WHAT TO DO WHEN YOU DON'T KNOW WHAT TO DO:
BAD HABITS & ADDICTIONS

Copyright © 2005 by Henry Cloud and John Townsend.

Published by Integrity Publishers, a division of Integrity Media, Inc.,
5250 Virginia Way, Suite 110, Brentwood, TN 37027.

HELPING PEOPLE WORLDWIDE EXPERIENCE *the* MANIFEST PRESENCE
of GOD.

All rights reserved. No portion of this book may be reproduced, stored
in a retrieval system, or transmitted in any form or by any means—
electronic, mechanical, photocopy, recording, or any other—except for
brief quotations in printed reviews, without the prior written permission of the publisher.

Published in association with Yates & Yates, LLP, Literary Agents,
Orange, California.

Unless otherwise indicated, Scripture quotations are taken from The
Holy Bible, New International Version (NIV), copyright ©1973, 1978,
1984, International Bible Society. Used by permission of Zondervan
Bible Publishers.

Other Scripture quotations are taken from the following sources:

The Holy Bible, New Living Translation (NLT), copyright ©1996.
Used by permission of Tyndale House Publishers, Inc., Wheaton,
Illinois. All rights reserved.

Cover and interior design: UDG | DesignWorks,
www.udgdesignworks.com

ISBN 1-59145-357-7

Printed in the United States of America

05 06 07 08 09   LBM   9 8 7 6 5 4 3 2 1

Contents

Prologue

Recently on our national radio talk show we received a call from Marian, a middle-class career woman who was on the verge of losing it all, even her husband and children. In a not-so-smart moment, she had "just once" tried crack cocaine. Drug use was totally out of character for this respected Midwestern mother, but because of the power of chemical addiction, she was not able to do cocaine "just once." The drug had instantly gripped her, and she suddenly found herself to be something that she never would have imagined—an addict. She had no idea what to do or where to turn.

Helpless, hopeless, and feeling terribly guilty, Marian turned to God. She made a commitment to being good, mustered up her will to stop the drug use, and began attending church. But doing the "God thing" was not working. Nothing was changing. Now believing that not even God would help her, she was more desperate than before.

Marian was not finding God; she was only finding religion. Big difference. Religion is about trying to be better and using "God language" to do it. If she had found God, she would have found help and strength beyond her own efforts. Instead, she seemed like a half-dead person trying to shock herself back to life with electric paddles.

God's way, we explained, does not depend on our willpower and commitment to transform a hopeless situation. He can raise people from the dead and create life where none exists. We said we wanted to see her in a program, surrounded by other addicts through whom God could provide his help and express his love and support. We asked Marian to abandon her effort to help herself by sheer human willpower and to reach out for God to meet her where she was. And we prayed for God to do a miracle for her.

Marian was willing to do all we suggested. She opened herself to God's help, and that's when the miracle began. Here's how it happened: We knew just the drug rehabilitation center she needed, but she didn't have the money to pay for it and had no idea how to get it. So we prayed that God would make a way.

Within minutes, the phone began ringing. People from all over the country called to say they felt God moving them to help pay for Marian's treatment. Money was pouring in, and we were certain that God had answered our prayer. But at the end of the program we were dismayed to find that we had come up short—$5,400 short, to be exact. But God was not through yet. The phone rang again, and a woman told us that she had received an inheritance and felt God moving her to give a gift for this woman's treatment.

"How much is your gift?" we asked.

"The inheritance was $54,000," she replied. "I want to give ten percent—$5,400."

We were ecstatic! God had indeed made a way. Within a short time Marian was in treatment and, as of this writing, she is doing great.

Little did Marian know that her call from the Midwest to a radio studio in California would land her in a treatment center in Arizona, paid for by people from several other states. Stories like Marian's tell us that God shows up in many ways and changes even the most hopeless situations. One of the most powerful lessons we can learn is that even when bad things happen and we don't know what to do about them, we can trust God to be present and working on our behalf, creating a path through the most painful wilderness. Even when the problem is of our own making.

The main obstacle to following God's way

through crises is failing to trust him. Most of us have little difficulty believing in God. But for some reason we balk when it comes to really trusting God. Our doubts rage like a rising river: *Will he come through for me? Can I depend on him?*

Trust is the bridge over that river. The way God makes for you means nothing until you step on the bridge and start walking. Trust is both an attitude and an action. You must follow your first small step with another and another. The more you act on your faith in God, the more you will see of his way for you.

God is active on your behalf, even when you cannot see it. Faith calls you to be active also. This may seem like a paradox. Am I doing it? Or is God doing it? The answer to both questions is yes. God will do what only he can do, and your job is to do what you can do. Marian could not kick her crack habit or find the money for treatment. God had to do all of that. She did not know what to do, but she acted by praying to him to do something, and by taking the steps he placed before her. That's faith.

The God who made a way for Marian is available to you now. He watches over all of the earth, with an ear attuned to all who desire him. As the psalmist said, "The LORD is near to all who call on him, to all who call on him in truth. He fulfills the desires of those who fear him; he hears their cry and saves them" (Psalm 145:18–19).

We don't believe you are reading this book by coincidence, any more than Marian tuned into our program that day by coincidence. And just as Marian's faith made her well as she followed God's directions, you will have the same experience when you exercise your faith in God by following the eight principles we will show you in the next section. Just as you would exercise faith in a doctor by following his instructions, by following God's instructions you can overcome the toughest addictions and worst habits. So join us as we show you how to follow God's way in your life.

PART I:
EIGHT PRINCIPLES TO GUIDE YOUR RECOVERY FROM ADDICTION

Most people cannot see God's way to recovery because they have difficulty believing there is a way. Their previous failures to win over their habit or addiction has left them feeling hopeless and not knowing what to do.

Well, there is good news. There is a way, and you can find it when you activate your faith in God by following eight principles in this section. We will have more to say specifically about overcoming addiction in the section that follows this one. These principles are foundation stones. You must lay them in your life so that you can build on them the structures you need to win over your problem.

Meaningful faith must be placed

in a real Person

who knows

the way for you and

promises to lead you on it.

That's God.

Begin Your Journey with God

When we speak of God, we don't mean some kind of vague, universal force; we mean a real person, complete with mind, will, and the power to act in our lives. So when we say that faith and trust will carry you to victory over your addictions, we're not talking about warm religious feelings or an exercise in positive thinking. Meaningful faith must be placed in a real Person who knows the way for you and promises to lead you on it. That's God. So our first principle for healing your addiction is to *begin your journey with God.* You can't do it without him.

Your need for God's help is no more a weakness than your need for air. We did not create ourselves, nor were we designed to create our own way in life. God wired us to depend on him. When you exercise faith in him, you position yourself to accomplish superhuman feats, which is what overcoming addiction requires. You are reaching beyond human strength and knowledge and tapping into God's infinite strength and knowledge.

Most of us, when we don't know what to do in the face of a difficult or painful situation, do one of two things. First, we repeat what didn't work before, but this time we try harder. Chronic dieters, for example, try to muster up just a little more will power, and "this time it will work." Second, we stop trying altogether. *I will never stop overeating, so what's the use?* The first reaction often spawns the second. Trying to get through life on your own limited strength and knowledge leads to futility and loss of hope.

But in God's economy, getting to the end of yourself is the beginning of hope. Jesus said, "God blesses those who realize their need for him" (Matthew 5:3 NLT). When you admit your helplessness and ask God for help, you transcend your own limitations and God's resources become available to you.

God's resources cannot be earned; they can only be received as a gift when we, in humility, acknowledge our need for our Creator. He's ready to get involved in your life. All you have to do is say yes to him. Then he will provide what you need to overcome even the worst, most entrenched and devastating addiction.

Sometimes his way will be truly miraculous, and sometimes it will involve a lot of work and change on your part. Often it won't be the way you thought you needed. But when God makes a way, it works.

People who

rise to the top seldom

get there alone.

They seek help.

❧

Choose Your Traveling Companions Wisely

When I (Henry) was a youngster, Jack Nicklaus was king of golf, and as an aspiring golfer, I thought he was almost a god. Then I heard that he consulted a golf pro for help on his swing. I was stunned. Teachers were for people who didn't know what they were doing. I have learned a lot since then. People who rise to the top seldom get there alone. They seek help.

This story illustrates our second principle of God's way of overcoming addictions: *Surround yourself with people who are committed to support*

One of the ways
God works is
through other
people.

you, encourage you, assist you, and pray for you.

One of the ways God works is through other people. Solomon said, "Two are better than one. . . . If one falls down, his friend can help him up. But pity the man who falls and has no one to help him up!" (Ecclesiastes 4:9–10). Often they will know exactly what to do when you don't. Some of these people will just show up in your life, sent at just the right time. Others you have to seek out. They can range from professionals to a neighbor or friend at church. Here are some important qualities to look for as you select your support team.

SUPPORT. In overcoming an addiction, you are pushing uphill. It can drain you of emotional, physical, and spiritual strength. You need the kind of person who will show up at your door anytime to help you.

LOVE. You need the safety net of people who love you deeply just as you are, faults included.

COURAGE. You will encounter risk and fear. When the task looks too daunting to face, your support team will build your courage.

FEEDBACK. You can't see yourself objectively. You need honest people who are not afraid to correct you when you are wrong.

WISDOM. You don't have all the wisdom and knowledge you need to make it. Look for wise people through whom God will speak to you.

EXPERIENCE. Seek out the experience of others who have been through addictions and know what you are going through.

MODELING. Often we don't know what to do because we have never seen it done. Seek out and learn from those who have recovered from addictions.

VALUES. Your value system will guide you as you turn your life around. We learn values from others, and others support us by enforcing values. Stay close to people who share your values; stay away from those who don't.

ACCOUNTABILITY. You need people who will monitor your progress and keep you on track. Look for people who will ask the tough questions: Where are you failing? What kind of help do you need?

You may already have in your life people who meet your need for support. If so, explain that you need them on your journey to recovery. Ask if they will be available to provide accountability, feedback, or support. They will probably feel honored and valued that you would ask.

If you run short of supportive friends, consider joining a structured support system, such as a Bible study group. Share with these people your struggle and ask for their prayers and input. You will be amazed how a loving support group will help you on your journey.

A key way out of despair is to
find the missing pieces of
wisdom and apply them
to your problem.

❦

Place High Value on Wisdom

Often we don't know what to do about our addiction because we lack vital information about its nature and its cure. A key way out of despair is to find these missing pieces of wisdom and apply them to our problem. God tells us that wisdom produces hope: "Know also that wisdom is sweet to your soul; if you find it, there is a future hope for you, and your hope will not be cut off" (Proverbs 24:14).

So our third principle for finding God's way through your addiction is this: *Recognize the value and need for the missing pieces of wisdom in your life; then ask God to show them to you.*

WISDOM COMES FROM GOD. James tells us to ask God for the wisdom we need: "If any of you lacks wisdom, he should ask God, who gives generously to all without finding fault . . ." (James 1:5). God knows what to do even when you don't. Ask him for answers and he will provide them.

GOD USES OTHERS. You may not know how to handle your situation, but there is somebody out there who does. Find that someone. Whenever I (Henry) am dealing with a difficult financial situation, I call a certain friend who has great wisdom in that area, and I lean on him for good advice. I have other people I call for other needs.

When facing an addiction, you are wise to seek out people who have knowledge, expertise, and experience in that area—people who have been there, done that, and gotten through it. Keep asking around until you find them.

SEEK STRUCTURED WISDOM. Usually dealing with an addiction requires more than good advice from friends or others. You also need structured and professional sources of wisdom. And there are a great number of services out there, including trained counselors, substance abuse programs, and even specialties in several areas of addiction. You don't need to reinvent the wheel for your situation. There is help available, already in place.

Don't use cost as an excuse not to take advantage of professional help. Yes, some programs are expensive, but many are free, and financial assistance is often available from the government and other agencies. Ferret out all your possibilities.

Here is a sampling of places to start looking:

- Professionals in your area of need

- Self-help groups

- Pastors

- Churches

- Community colleges

- Seminars

- Books, tapes, and videos

- Workshops

- Retreats

One caution: Make sure the resources you uncover are authentic. Get referrals from people you trust—your friends, your support group, your doctor, or your pastor.

THE ORDER OF THINGS. God has put you in a universe of order. Things work because of the laws God set in place at creation. Part of the way for you to win over your addiction has already been made in how he created life to work. Your task is to find the wisdom that is already there. So search for his wisdom with all your strength and apply it wholeheartedly.

Leave Your Baggage Behind

We all hate dragging a million pieces of luggage through a crowded airport. What if you had to tote a couple of suitcases, backpacks, and carry-on bags everywhere you went? It would weigh you down and hold you back.

It's the same when overcoming an addiction. Emotional baggage can weigh you down and hold you back. Our fourth principle for finding God's way to addiction recovery is to *leave your baggage behind.*

By baggage we mean bad stuff from the past. We've all experienced difficult events and relationships, emotional hurts, divorces, serious mistakes, tragic accidents, or loss of a loved one. Ideally, these events are resolved as they happen. But often pain is stuffed instead of dealt with; offenders are not forgiven; fears are not confronted; conflicts are not resolved, leaving us with past feelings and patterns of behavior that impact the present. That's baggage. You can be sure that some of your baggage is directly related to your addiction, and that you can't be fully healed until you deal with it.

Here are five practical tips for helping you discard baggage.

1. AGREE THAT YOU HAVE A PAINFUL PAST. Acknowledge that painful things have happened to you that were not resolved. If you don't work through them, they will prevent your recovery. So the first step is to confess to yourself and to God that you have these issues.

2. Include others in your healing and grieving. Seek from others the care and healing you need to resolve these issues. Pouring out your hurt to others who love you opens the door to comfort, encouragement, healing, and support.

3. Receive forgiveness. Getting rid of baggage means being free of the guilt and shame of past failures and sins. God will forgive you for anything you have ever done, no matter how bad. The Bible promises, "For as high as the heavens are above the earth, so great is his love for those who fear him; as far as the east is from the west, so far has he removed our transgressions from us" (Psalm 103:11–12).

Your past failures and mistakes may also have alienated you from certain people. You must go to them, humbly confess your wrong, and receive forgiveness. Once you know you are forgiven, accepted, and loved, you can then re-enter life and begin moving on.

> You still carry pain, anger, and perhaps hatred. You must forgive these people.

4. FORGIVE OTHERS. Some of your baggage may be hurts you received from others. You still carry pain, anger, and perhaps hatred. You must forgive these people. Take your cue from God, who has forgiven you. If you don't forgive, resentment will eat away at your heart. When you forgive another, you release that person from your right to exact punishment and retribution from them. As well, you release your own baggage of pain and resentment in the process.

5. SEE YOURSELF THROUGH NEW EYES. Another kind of baggage is the distorted view of ourselves we learned in past relationships or situations. We tend to see ourselves through the eyes of others who are important to us. And depending on whether that view is positive or negative, we either feel valued or devalued. A realistic self-view will be balanced, recognizing strengths as well as weaknesses and growth areas.

Find this view by seeing yourself through God's eyes, for he loves you unconditionally and values you highly. Add to this the view you get from those who love you as God does. Let this *new you* replace the distorted picture that has caused you such grief.

Holding on to the baggage of the past will disable your search for victory over addiction. Ask God to help you leave it behind.

In your life,

the buck stops with you.

When addressing any problem,

you need to step up

to the plate and take charge.

☙

Own Your Faults and Weaknesses

I n your life, the buck stops with you. When addressing a problem like addiction, you need to step up to the plate and take charge. It's your job to do what God gives you to do. And it's your job to accept the blame for the failures that are truly your own failures, not someone else's. Our fifth principle for God's way to recovery is that you *take responsibility for your life, own up to your faults, and accept blame where it is justified.*

The apostle Paul wrote, "Continue to work out your salvation with fear and trembling, for it

> Sometimes we have to take responsibility for situations that are not our fault.

is God who works in you to will and to act according to his good purpose" (Philippians 2:12–13). Now that God has saved you, it's your responsibility to live a life that reflects him. But notice that you are not alone in your efforts. God is there with you, empowering you. And this partnership between you and him accomplishes your goal.

Sometimes we have to take responsibility for situations that are not our fault. The man who is unfairly laid off must own up to the situation and start looking for another job. The abused wife must seek counseling.

Determining who is at fault isn't as important as determining who will do something about it. The latter "who" is you. Whoever is at fault, what matters is taking ownership to correct the problem. As you do, God will show you his way.

When we take ownership for what happens in our lives, we are empowered to make changes— to develop plans, tackle situations, and right wrongs. People who take charge of their lives are active people with real initiative. Ownership also frees us from false hopes, from discouragement and passivity, and to take risks and test-drive possible solutions.

When you take ownership and invite God to move in, he does it. He will get involved in moving you to success in overcoming your addiction. Our role is to seek him, take charge of our own circumstances, and trust him to do for us what only he can do.

Welcome your problems as

gifts from God

to help you

become a better person.

Embrace Problems
as Gifts

Some people hit a problem and stop dead in their tracks—they feel stuck and hopeless. All they want is to get rid of it as soon as possible. Other people find something useful in problems. They ask, "What can I learn from this experience? What does God want to change in me?" This is our sixth principle for finding God's way out of addiction: *Welcome your problems as gifts from God to help you become a better person.*

There's nothing wrong with trying to solve a problem and alleviate the pain. But instead of rushing to the most immediate fix, we must use the problem to see our lives from God's perspective and find God's way through it.

And God's perspective is quite different. We might compare it to how differently a physician and a patient view pain. You come to the doctor in agony wanting a shot or a pill to make the pain go away. And you want it *now*. But your physician knows your pain is a sign of a deeper problem. He prescribes even more pain: surgery and physical therapy.

It's a choice all of us have to make at some point: You can demand immediate relief, knowing that your problem will recur. Or you can go through the healing process and resolve the problem once and for all. That's the choice you face when dealing with an addiction. God loves you, and like your physician, he is less concerned about your immediate comfort than about your long-term health.

The Bible tells us, "Consider it pure joy, my brothers, whenever you face trials of many kinds, because you know that the testing of your faith develops perseverance" (James 1:2–3). God's way is not *out* of your problem but *through* it. That's how we learn from our difficulties and find God's way.

When facing your addiction, you first need to look upward, toward God. He is like a storm raining down on a stagnant stream clogged with debris. As the torrent floods the stream, the debris is broken up and the flow resumes.

Second, you must look *inward*. Let God take you on a journey into yourself. He will shine a lantern of truth into the recesses of your heart, illuminating attitudes, wounds, hurts, weaknesses, and perspectives where you need to submit to his touch.

Problems are also a gift in that they help us *normalize* pain—to expect it as a regular part of life. We tend to think that bad things shouldn't happen to us, and we react in anger, denial, or despair when they do. But this doesn't alter the reality of the pain.

You must give up your protest about the unfairness of your problems and come to a place of acceptance. Only then can you learn what choices, paths, lessons, and opportunities are available to you. Accept pain as part of life. Accept that you don't have all the answers. Acceptance helps us to adapt to the way things really are, and to trust God.

Our problems help us identify with Jesus's sufferings. He loves us deeply, and our rebellion hurts him. But instead of finding a way out, he works through it. While he redeems, restores, and forgives us, he suffers. But he endures it because it's the only way. That is our model for dealing with pain. Identifying with his pain draws us closer to him, to see life as it really is and patiently take whatever steps are necessary to resolve the problem. Following the pattern of Jesus deepens and matures us.

Don't tolerate your addiction, but don't ask God to just make it vanish instantly. Work through it God's way, and accept the gift of what you learn from the process.

Take Life as It Comes

I (John) have a bone disease called osteopenia. My bones are too porous, and they break easier than normal bones. I am on a special diet and a regimen of bone-strengthening exercises. I get an annual x-ray to check my progress. I would love to get more frequent progress reports, but bones change too slowly for that. The waiting is difficult, but it has taught me that I am not the master of time. I can't speed it up. I must let time have its way.

Our seventh principle for following God's way relates to what I am learning through my osteopenia: *We must allow time for God to work.* Though I believe that God performs instantaneous miracles, it seems that his norm is a time-consuming process. Therefore, you must allow time for his process to happen.

Still, it's not easy to wait. When things don't happen quickly, we tend to become impatient, frustrated, and ready to give up. However, those who insist on shortcuts and quick fixes tend to repeat the same problems over and over, getting nowhere.

You've heard the saying "Time heals all wounds." Time heals nothing in and of itself. It's futile to wait passively for God to change circumstances, for help to appear, or for your feelings to change. Such inaction will stick you in a holding pattern where you'll become discouraged when healing doesn't occur. You don't simply wait for a sprained knee to heal. You get a brace and do the physical therapy. Time is the context for our involvement in the process. When you invite God into your life and participate with him in the process, you will begin to see results. So do your part. Seek help and surround yourself with support and accountability. The more engaged you are, the less you will feel the pressure of time.

As nature has seasons, so do our lives. Solomon wrote, "There is a time for everything, and a season for every activity under heaven" (Ecclesiastes 3:1). We can better understand God's timing when we understand the seasons of our lives and identify which we are in.

WINTER. Cold weather and hard ground make things appear dead and unfruitful, but winter can be a very productive time. It's a time to clear out the deadwood, debris, and stones that will hinder future growth; to mend fences and repair broken machinery; to plan and prepare for the growing seasons.

Arrange your schedule and set goals. Research the resources you need, such as a support team, organizations and programs, and counselors. Use winter to prepare.

SPRING. It's a time of new beginnings and fresh hope. You plow the soil, add fertilizer and supplements, plant seeds, and irrigate. You care for the fragile shoots that appear, keeping the garden free of destructive pests.

In the spring of your life, you implement the plans you made in the winter. See a counselor, enter a program, or join a group.

SUMMER. In summer the fields are lush with healthy plants. It's a season for maintenance and protection of what you began in the spring. Don't be lulled into inactivity because good things are happening. Stay with the program; keep working at what God has given you to do.

FALL. At harvesttime you reap what you have sown. You experience and enjoy the benefits of your work.

In the fall of personal growth, you see victory in your battle with addiction. It's a time of celebration and gratitude. It's a time to give back to God and others something of what you have received.

We would all rather skip the work of winter, spring, and summer and enjoy the harvest of fall all the time. But the only way to reap a bountiful harvest is to make good use of your time in each season.

Getting to

know God and

loving him

with everything you are

is a lifelong journey.

❧

Love God with All You Are

God loves you unconditionally and has a way for you through your addiction. Following his way is a matter of love on your part. Our eighth principle for following God's way is to *love him passionately with every area of your life*.

Jesus said, "Love the Lord your God with all your heart and with all your soul and with all your mind. This is the first and greatest commandment" (Matthew 22:37–38). Loving God is the greatest commandment because it encompasses all the others. If we love God, connect to him,

> Immerse yourself in God's love, and you will find his way to victory.

and do what honors him, we will find that we are also doing what is best for us. Immerse yourself in his love, and you will find his way to victory.

Here are a few facets of your life where love for God must take the lead.

VALUES. Our values determine what is important to us. Loving God means what is important to him should be important to you.

PASSIONS. These deep urges and drives make us feel alive. Let your love for God fuel your passions.

EMOTIONS. No matter how you feel in your situation—afraid, anxious, sad, or angry—ask God to reach inside you with his love so that you will be able to feel your feelings in ways that help you grow and move on.

TALENTS. Love God with all your strengths, skills, and abilities. As you do, God will use you to make a way for others.

Think of the dearest, closest, most loving relationship in your life. What characterizes this relationship? You are probably very open and vulnerable with each other. You know each other's secrets, fears, and desires. You take risks with each other. You need and depend on each other. And this relationship makes you feel alive.

Our best human relationships are only a frail picture of the loving, intimate relationship you can enjoy with God. Learning to love him with everything you are is a lifelong journey. And the more of yourself you open up to him, the more God is able to help you through your addiction.

Loving God is saying to him, "Do whatever you need to do in my life." This gives him access to every part of you that needs his love, grace, and support.

You may feel connected to God in your head, theologically, but not in your heart, emotionally. Or the converse may be true. Either way, begin to bring those aspects of your soul and life to his grace, so that all of you is being loved and supported by God himself.

If you ever need God's way in your life, it's when you are suffering with an addiction. God has the will and the resources to put your life back together again. "He heals the brokenhearted and binds up their wounds" (Psalm 147:3). However, you must bring your addiction to God in order to experience his love and healing.

God is all about love, and he wants us to be all about love too. The more you make everything you are accessible to him, the more you can grow, be healed, and find his way. Be sure you are not hiding your addiction from God. Love God with your heart, soul, mind, and strength, and let his love set you free.

PART II:
BAD HABITS AND ADDICTIONS

What does the word *addiction* mean to you? Our hunch is that there are almost as many answers to that question as there are people who answer it. For instance, people have said:

- "There's no such thing as an addiction. People who engage in addictive behaviors don't have a disease; they simply fail to exercise control over their actions."

- "Only substances can be addicting."

- "Only behaviors like gambling and drinking can be addicting."

- "Almost any kind of activity, such as shopping or exercise, can be addicting."

The more we talk about addictions, the more the term seems to lose its meaning. It becomes difficult to know if we are even talking about the same thing.

So we are going to make some assumptions about addiction and then speak to those assumptions. *If you picked up this book because there is something in your life that you can't stop, and you think you have an addiction, then you should look to what follows for answers.* We want to help you.

For that reason, we have chosen to talk about addictions using the broadest sense of the word. Although there are some technical inaccuracies with this approach, it allows all of us to identify with the problem, to some degree—and all of us can benefit from living our lives in a way that enables us to be connected to God and to others.

In light of that, here is the definition we will use: *Addiction is an inability to stop a repeated and compulsive use of an activity, behavior, or substance in spite of its negative consequences.*

With that definition, a lot of us are in trouble! It does not include the things that we normally associate with being an addict—being out on the street, penniless, and friendless. Most of our culture's disturbing pictures of addicts focus on the devastating final stages of severe abuse of such substances as alcohol or heroin. When those addictions go untreated over a long period, people can lose all they have, even their lives. Many of us think of an addict only as someone who is down and out and has lost everything—job, home, and family.

As a result of this picture, many people who struggle with uncontrollable habits find it easy to lie to themselves. Even though they are unable to give up a substance or behavior despite its negative consequences, they think that since they function well in their jobs, since they have homes, families, a bank account, and friends, they don't have an addiction. But they are wrong. It's very possible to be a high performer and still be out of control with how you use money, food, sex, alcohol, exercise, or many other things.

I (Henry) talked to a woman just today who is in recovery for what she terms "romance addiction." She was addicted to romantic relationships despite their negative consequences for her. As we talked, she told me about her father. She said that he was an alcoholic, "but no one would ever know." When I asked her what she meant, she said that her dad did well in his job, but every day he came home and had several martinis to medicate his stress and his loneliness. When his wife confronted him about his drinking, he denied that he had a problem, saying that his drinking was not interfering with his life. Yet it was. He was becoming more and more detached from his family and had very little meaningful interaction with his daughter. He was just too medicated to engage with her day after day.

What was the result? She grew up totally detached from her father and began craving attention from men as a way to validate her as a person and as a woman. She found herself in relationships with men who did not value her other than for sex. She became pregnant by a man who would not commit to a relationship with her, and she had an abortion. In the midst of trying to win the love of these men, she was losing more and more of herself and all that mattered to her.

Fortunately, God is making a way for this woman to break that cycle and find a deeply satisfying life, and that same God can make a way for you as well when you don't know what to do.

THE PICTURE OF ADDICTION

What do most addictions look like? In general, most addicts follow this two-step path:

1. THEY BEGIN WITH A BEHAVIOR THAT BRINGS THEM PLEASURE. This can be pleasure in and of itself, engaged in for its own sake simply for the good feelings it brings, like what happens when

people use drugs for the first time. Or the pleasure may be one indulged not for its own sake, but rather to achieve a feeling of relief from a bad state of mind or emotional distress. For instance, a woman on the way home from a stressful job may find that when she stops off at the mall and spends a lot of money, or stops at the local bar and has a few drinks, her stress diminishes. The pleasure that she finds is the pleasure of relief from some sort of pain, anxiety, or other distress. However, after the effects of the pleasurable experience have worn away, her body and mind will come back to the state they were in before the relief provided by the addictive behavior, and she will likely desire to go back to that state of pleasure. In other words, the substance or behavior has become self-reinforcing.

2. THEY BECOME PSYCHOLOGICALLY OR PHYSI-CALLY DEPENDENT ON THE BEHAVIOR OR SUB-STANCE. They begin to need the pleasure-induc-ing substance or behavior, often in ever-increas-

ing amounts to get the same effect or relief. I (Henry) know a man who occasionally smokes cigars. I asked him once if he had ever had any problem with smoking, if it had ever gotten out of control. He told me that early on in his business career, he would sometimes bum a cigarette from a coworker on his way out the door at the end of the day. He liked the relaxing effect of smoking and thought it was just an occasional pleasure. Then he noticed something happening. On days when he was particularly stressed, he found himself wanting to go find the person and get a cigarette. He realized that he desired to smoke as a tension reliever. When he saw that beginning to happen, he quit smoking. His occasional use of a highly addicting drug had escalated and become self-reinforcing as a stress reliever.

However, most people fail to recognize that this kind of thing is happening, and they continue to do what makes them feel better. In fact, in a lot of circles, their behavior is even normalized.

Many people feel it's normal and acceptable to seek sexual release or to drink alcohol to blow off some steam. They do not recognize the warning signs, and so they continue the behavior. They're like the proverbial frog in the kettle that doesn't notice the gradual increase in the water temperature until it is boiling. The addictive behavior gradually takes over more of their soul, but at the same time it numbs them so that they don't even know it.

Then typically, something negative happens to the person—some sort of negative consequence of the behavior emerges. It could be guilt, shame, or someone getting upset with him. But still he doesn't stop. He continues the behavior in spite of the negative consequences. At this point, addiction has definitely set in. *Addiction becomes apparent when a person doesn't acknowledge the negative consequence, explains it away, or acknowledges it and yet is unable to stop.* Many addicts make repeated promises, either to themselves or to others, that they will not engage in the addictive behavior anymore, and yet they can't keep those promises. They have lost self-control and have become enslaved to the behavior. They no longer have a choice.

It is all downhill from there, as the negative consequences usually increase. Addicts often have relational difficulties, such as tension in a marriage or with friends or family. They have performance difficulties, such as the inability to do their job or other tasks well. They often experience financial consequences, as addictions sometimes become expensive or can erode a person's financial well-being in other ways, such as the ability to earn money or to manage it wisely. As the cycle of addiction becomes more and more pervasive, many addicts suffer internal consequences, such as mood disturbances, depression, guilt, anxiety, or shame.

Yet despite all of these debilitating consequences, the addict can't seem to stop the behavior.

Sex addicts lose marriages and catch diseases but still find themselves unable to stop. Gambling addicts lose their life savings yet continue to try to find more money to support their habit, often in problematic ways, such as dangerous loans or going into credit-card debt. Alcoholics keep drinking even after being confronted by their families or after being diagnosed with liver problems. Food addicts may gain a lot of weight, risking their health and encountering other consequences that limit their quality of life internally, physically, relationally, sexually, and otherwise.

Of course, there are occasional exceptions to the general picture. Some people are able to control things for periods of time, sometimes even for long periods. Yet, when they do engage in the behavior, it goes immediately out of control and becomes destructive to themselves or others. Even though the behavior is not continual, its repeated bouts result in the same kinds of negative consequences. People who engage in such addictive behavior intermittently are often called *binge addicts.*

The hallmark of all addictions is that the person has lost control and is experiencing negative consequences as a result.

Sadly, many of the activities that people become addicted to are things that God has designed to be a part of life, such as food, money, and sex. The problem comes when these things become consuming, so much so that the person loses his or her ability to control the use of them and becomes a slave of the behavior or substance. As the apostle Paul says, "'Everything is permissible for me'—but not everything is beneficial. 'Everything is permissible for me'—but I will not be mastered by anything" (1 Corinthians 6:12).

The Greek word translated "mastered" is a word that means "having power or control." In other words, the person has lost control or power of his or her own life in that area, and the addiction has taken control. Likewise, when Paul says

> When we admit we are powerless to change, we can turn to God for help.

not to be "addicted to much wine" (Titus 2:3), the Greek word translated "addicted" is a word that means to be "brought under bondage or become a servant to." God seems to recognize that people can become addicted and that a person can actually become powerless over things in life. The loss of control is ultimately the kernel of addiction. Paradoxically, the loss of control is also the beginning of change—and of hope. When we admit that we are powerless to change, we can turn to God for help.

LET'S GET HONEST

Now that we've talked about addictions in general and how they affect a person, let's talk about you. Answer the following questions:

- Is there something in your life that has gotten control of you? Something that's beginning to show itself as a problem, either to you or to others? Are you unwilling or unable to give up that behavior, despite its negative consequences? Do you find yourself making excuses or trying to convince yourself or someone else that the behavior is really not that big a deal? Or excusing the behavior by pointing out others who have a much greater problem than you do?

• Do you go through periods of withdrawal? Do you have cravings that can be satisfied only by the substance or the behavior? Do you find that the substance or behavior does not ultimately satisfy because you need it again or need more? (This is called "tolerance." It is the need for more in order to produce the same result.)

• Do you obsess about the behavior more and more? Do you organize more and more of your life so that you can engage in the behavior? Is it affecting the amount of time and energy you have for the things and the people that are important to you?

- Do you often feel guilty or ashamed of the behavior and yet find that you are unable to stop? Do you make promises to yourself or someone else that you will quit or cut back and yet do not? Is the behavior at odds with your value system, and yet you continue? Do you tell yourself that you really could quit if you wanted to but you just don't try?

- Have others noticed the effects of the behavior? Do they mention it or get upset by it? When they do mention it, do you get defensive?

- Do you feel better when engaged in the behavior and then find that other things in life cannot bring you the same degree of pleasure, excitement, involvement, or momentary relief that the behavior does? Do you engage in it more than you intended or expected to? Is the behavior affecting your health or performance in life, relationships, or work? Are you having emotional problems, mood swings, or thinking difficulties as a result of the behavior?

- Have you lost consciousness or memory because of a substance? Do you disappear from others and hide your behavior or use of a substance? Do you find yourself lying about what you are doing or not doing? Do you try to cover up what you do?

These questions address some of the signs of addiction. If you answered yes to any of these questions, then you may have a problem.

Perhaps you're wondering why some people can enjoy many addictive substances and behaviors and still remain in control, yet others can't. After all, no one goes out and says, "I want to become an alcoholic." No one chooses to become addicted to pornography, shopping, sex, gambling, cocaine, or any other substance or behavior. Why do these things sometimes take control of people's lives?

WHY PEOPLE GET ADDICTED

People get addicted to things for a variety of reasons. The overarching reason is that we are fallen humans—separated from God and life—and as a result we find ourselves out of control in a lot of ways. Yet first let's summarize some of the specific forces that drive an addiction.

Some people seem to have a particular genetic makeup that is prone to addiction toward certain substances, such as alcohol.

Environmental forces may work. People who are injured by malfunctions in significant relationships or grow up in families where certain negative relational and life patterns are modeled may not develop the coping skills needed to deal with emotional hurts and injuries. Some, thus scarred, turn to an addiction to medicate their pain.

We live in an ongoing spiritual battle in this universe between the forces of darkness and the forces of light. Living forces of evil really do exist, though they are invisible to us, and they try to do everything possible to tempt humans to pursue darkness instead of God and his ways. As a result, some people make seemingly innocuous choices that take them further away from the light and down a road of destruction, such as a one-time experiment with drugs or a choice to turn away from God's ways and experiment with a behavior that brings momentary pleasure. Many addicts to drugs, sex, gambling, and pornography will tell you that such dangerous choices and seemingly innocent "first times" can trap you and lead you into total darkness.

The emotional makeup and personal dynamics of some people can predispose them toward an addiction that might not snare another person. These dynamics include:

- an internal sense of relational isolation and alienation, resulting in loneliness and a hunger for love;

- a sense of powerlessness in life—a sense of being controlled by others, circumstances, and forces bigger than themselves;

- inability to gain mastery and thus develop a sense of personal power that is adequate to cope with the ups and downs of life and deal with other people;

- feelings of shame, guilt, "badness," failure, or other negative attitudes toward themselves and their innate worth;

- unresolved losses and failures and the inability to deal with them;

- unresolved trauma, hurt, abuse, and pain of all kinds;

- feelings of inferiority and inability to develop competencies in life;

- feelings of being dominated by others and not living up to their standards; and

- difficult times in life becoming overwhelming because of the ineffectiveness of one's coping mechanisms and skills.

While all the conditions on this list can be factors in the cause of addiction, they are all symptoms of another, deeper condition. It is the spiritual condition of being "alienated" from God and his life as he created us to live it. When we are cut off from him and his life, the Bible says that we become subject to addiction. Listen to how Paul describes it:

So I tell you this, and insist on it in the Lord, that you must no longer live as the Gentiles do, in the futility of their thinking. They are darkened in their understanding and separated from the life of God because of the ignorance that is in them due to the hardening of their hearts. Having lost all sensitivity, they have given themselves over to sensuality so as to *indulge in every kind of impurity, with a continual lust for more.*

—EPHESIANS 4:17–19, emphasis ours

When we become "darkened in our understanding" and "separated from the life of God," then we find ourselves in a lost state. Missing God in our lives, we seek to fill the vacuum by craving other things that will never satisfy. We experience a "continual lust for more." This craving drives us to want just one more drink, one more experience, one more sexual encounter, one more pizza, one more purchase. The desire is continual, which means that it is never completely satisfied and does not go away with the experience of the behavior we engage in to alleviate it.

This is a downward, futile, destructive cycle because it causes us to become separated from God and his life, even when we are among people who are "spiritual." A part of the soul is disconnected from God and his life, or from the resources and healing experiences of others around us who, if we would let them, could help us meet our deepest need in ways that are truly satisfying—the things that can truly reveal God's way.

If separation from God and his life is the cause, then reconciliation to God and his life is the answer. That is how to follow God's way for anyone with an addiction. He truly can set slaves free.

THE WAY OUT

Jeri had been enslaved to binge eating for a long time. Her doctor had sent her to counseling because he feared greatly for her health. She was extremely

> Yet that is part of addiction—the belief that one is really able to overcome the problem.

overweight and had a history of heart disease in her family. So naturally he was quite concerned about her. She had tried many times before to control her eating through dieting. She would always lose some weight at first, but eventually she would give up and quit, only to have the weight that she had lost return, with a few extra pounds on top of it all. She didn't know what else to do. Despair had given way to detachment, and she found herself in a lonely pattern. She had given up. Yet the doctor had gotten her attention by explaining the seriousness of her situation, and she now feared for her very life.

When Jeri came to our clinic, the first thing we had to do was "cure" her of her commitment to dieting. If that sounds crazy, read on. She came in mistakenly believing that all she needed to overcome her eating problem was to have more resolve and willpower. She believed that if she made a strong enough commitment, then she would be able to manage her eating. This is not the way to work against addiction. Jeri had to learn that addiction was by definition *the inability to stop.* In other words, she had to learn to admit that she was powerless over her addiction and totally helpless to stop. You would think that after gaining a few hundred pounds and after many failed efforts at dieting, Jeri would have seen that she did not stand a chance of changing by herself. Yet that is part of addiction—the belief that one really is able to overcome the problem.

Next, Jeri had to learn that she had not truly reached out to God as the Source of power in her life of addiction. She had "prayed" about her problem many times, but that is very different than leaning on God as a source of power *in the addiction itself.* She had to learn that when temptation came, she had to pray and ask God at that moment for the strength to know what to do to flee the temptation.

Then, she had to learn that God also gives us strength through other people. She began to see that part of the reason she had failed before was that she had tried to go it alone. She had thought because she had joined diet groups emphasizing group support, that she was getting all the support she needed. She discovered that in moments of weakness, when she was feeling loneliness or self-pity, she needed to be able to call a few people. She needed a "buddy system." She learned to reach out to God and to a buddy and to talk things out rather than using food to make herself feel better.

How well we remember the day when this insight hit her. She came to a group early that morning and said that the night before, she had been tempted to binge. "Now I get what you guys have been talking about," she said.

"What do you mean?" we asked.

"Well, last night I found myself craving some serious food. I was just about to give in when I remembered what you had said. There were three things: First, I needed to reach out to God. So I prayed and asked him to help me get through it and to show me what was going on. Second, you said that my cravings were not really for food, but had something to do with how I was feeling inside. Third, at those times I could not just depend on myself, but I had to reach out to someone else.

"So I asked God to help, and then I called Regina [another group member] and told her that I was struggling. As we talked, I began to feel really sad. And the more I talked, the sadder I got. I felt this really deep aloneness that I never had felt before. *This is not working*, I thought. But Regina told me just to keep talking, and I did. Then, slowly, the sad feeling went away. And the weird thing was that after that conversation, I was not hungry anymore, but I had not eaten anything. I think I am getting it!" she exclaimed with obvious excitement.

As Jeri continued to work on things, she found that there were other dynamics driving her eating. She also had a fear of getting close to men because of some past abuse that she had suffered. She had subconsciously gained a lot of weight as a way of keeping men safely at a distance. She gradually became aware of these things that triggered her desire to eat, and she had to learn another way to express that pain instead of "eating it away."

In time Jeri came to understand that she had a few character flaws as well. She was not as honest as she thought she was. She was indirect with people and then held grudges and bitterness toward them instead of talking things out directly, offering forgiveness, and resolving conflict. She had always been a "nice" person, but that niceness was covering a lot of anger and resentment, and her true feelings would come out in her tendency to talk about people behind their backs. She had to learn to repent of that kind of indirect, hurtful behavior and to offer forgiveness and resolve conflict.

Jeri went back to school and started a new business, which became successful. She was soon hired as a consultant and was really thrilled that she was able to exercise her gifts and talents, overcoming a longstanding belief that she was "stupid" and unable to do anything significant. Now "significant" people were paying her to help them.

Oh, and one more thing: Jeri lost half of her weight—and we do not mean half of her goal weight or half of the weight that she was supposed to lose. No, we mean *literally half of her body weight.* She went from 300 to 150 pounds. This was not as a result of a diet. She lost the weight as a result of getting reconnected to God and his life.

Here are the steps Jeri took to overcome her addiction:

- She got to the end of herself, the end of her own strength, and didn't know what to do about her addiction. She admitted her power-lessness.

- She found the strength she needed in reaching out to God.

- She found strength from God in reaching out to God's people.

- She overcame her aloneness and isolation through learning how to be vulnerable and to connect with others—this healed the pain that her eating was serving to medicate.

- She grew in her character, learning how to be honest, to be responsible, and to set good boundaries with others instead of being so passive and powerless.

- She grieved a lot of hurt.

- She forgave a lot of people and gave up a lot of bitterness.

- She developed her talents, reached out, took some risks, and grew a life of work and service.

- She learned to pray at a deeper, more realistic, and more dependent level.

- She began to study the Bible in a different way, not as religious obligation but as the place to find the wisdom that was healing her.

- She learned new interpersonal skills for building better relationships.

- She worked out conflicts with people, asked for forgiveness, and made amends.

- She learned to reach out to people at the critical times when she needed help.

- She lost the weight—150 pounds of it!

These steps map the path that God prescribes and that Jeri took. She got to the end of herself, reached out to God, and with his help got recon-nected to him and his life. He healed her, removed things from her soul and character that were hurting her, and built into her life some dynamic new things that she did not possess before going into her recovery. Through spiritual growth, her addiction was overcome.

FROM HOPE TO CERTAINTY FOR YOU TOO

If some part of your life is out of control and resulting in negative consequences, you may be struggling with an addiction. If so, you are a can-didate for recovery. Here is a summary of the steps you can take to find help and healing. You will notice that many of them are the same as the twelve steps of Alcoholics Anonymous:

1. Admit to yourself, to God, and to another trusted person that you are out of control and this addiction has gotten the best of you. Admit that you are powerless on your own to fix it.

2. Ask God for forgiveness for whatever you have done, and claim it. Receive it as true and real, and get rid of all self-condemnation.

3. Believe that God can help you, reach out to him, and totally submit yourself to his care, guidance, direction, and strength. Submit and commit yourself to total obedience to whatever he shows you to do.

4. Take an ongoing inventory of all that is wrong inside yourself, as well as between you and others. Broaden the scope of the self-investigation to include all that you have done wrong. Confess it to God and to someone else that you trust.

5. Continually ask God to show you any problem or deficiency in your life that you need to work on. And when he does tell you, follow through and work on it.

6. Go to everyone you have hurt and ask for forgiveness and make amends to them. Be judicious in doing this and make exceptions where bringing up buried things from the past might harm the person.

7. Seek God deeply. Ask him what he wants you to do; ask him for the power to do it, and then follow through in total obedience.

8. Reach out to others for help in overcoming your addictive behavior—especially to others who have gone through the problem and experienced victory.

9. Be alert and identify all the triggers that get your addictive behavior started. Then when they occur, that's the time to reach out. Do not ever underestimate the need to reach out. Recognition of this need is why some addicts, especially in the beginning, go to multiple meetings every day and have a sponsor who they can call at any time.

10. Dig deeply and discover inside yourself the hurts and pains that you are trying to medicate with your addiction and seek to have them healed. Find out what you are lacking inside and begin to reach out and receive the love and strengthening that you need.

11. Do not try to do all of this alone. Join a support system, and maybe attend every day for a few months. Line up a few buddies you can call on every day for a while, and any time you need them later.

12. Find out what relational skills you need to develop, improve, or repair in order to make your relationships work. Work on these skills and take risks in order to relate to people better.

13. Forgive everyone who has ever hurt you.

14. Assess yourself to discover what talents you have and develop them. Put them to work pursuing your deepest dreams and goals.

15. Simplify your life so that it has less stress, and make sure that you are getting adequate rest and recreation and taking care of yourself, mentally, emotionally, and spiritually.

16. Join a structured group that will provide the discipline you will need to accomplish all of this.

17. Study God's Word and other spiritual writings that will teach you how to apply it.

18. Stay humble, be honest, and remember that spiritual growth and recovery are for a lifetime, not just for a season.

19. If you are addicted to a substance, seek medical help as well. In the beginning of your treatment for substance abuse, it is possible that you will go through withdrawal or other serious medical condi-

tions. Make sure that you have the professional supervision and counsel to do this safely.

20.   See your addiction not as the central problem but as a symptom of a life that is not planted and growing in God. Get into recovery as a total life overhaul, not just to fix a symptom.

It does not matter what you are addicted to—a substance, a person, a behavior, or something else. It does not matter how long you have been addicted. It does not matter how severe the consequences. When you don't know what to do about it, God will provide a way. All you have to do is to stop trying to tell yourself to be strong, admit that you are weak, and get into his system of recovery. The plan works if you work the plan. The strength will not come from you but from God. Yet you have to go to him with your weakness and join his program in order to receive his

The strength
will not come
from you
but from God

strength. We encourage you to do that and to discover, like millions before you, that no matter what your situation, God can help you make a way out of your addiction.

PART III:
BEGIN YOUR JOURNEY TODAY

You are near the end of this book, but you are only at the beginning of the journey God is making for you to overcome your addiction. You may have come to this book not knowing what to do in the face of your problem. We have shown you that God has a way for you, and we have tried to prepare you to walk in that way. In the earlier sections we filled your pack with supplies and put a map in your hands. Now it's time for you to hit the trail. As you do, we leave you with three final words of advice.

WALK IN GRACE. Your first step on the journey, and every subsequent step, is a step into God's grace. Simply put, grace is God's *unmerited favor*. This means that God is on your side. He wants you to resolve your addiction and is committed to work in you, with you, and through you to accomplish it. God loves you completely, and he's going with you every step of the way. He will be your biggest cheerleader.

STEP OUT IN FAITH. You need two strong legs to complete a strenuous hike—right, left, right, left, one after the other. Similarly, in your journey with God, faith is a two-step process. It is both an *attitude* and an *action*. You believe God loves you, but you need to love him in return. You know God will speak to you, but you need to listen attentively. You have faith that God will guide you and protect you, but you need to follow him and submit to his care. Whenever you take a step of *faith* in God, follow it with a step of *action*.

STAY ON THE TRAIL. Now that your feet are moving, let's take one last look at the trail ahead. This is the way God has made for you. It may be strenuous in trying times, but it is full of discovery and wonder. And the destination is well worth the effort. Here are ten key reminders that will help keep you on the trail and moving forward.

1. Set goals. What do you want God to do for you? Decide now, and be specific. Make your goal as clear and concise as possible so you can envision it, pray about it, and decide on a specific strategy to reach it.

2. Record progress. Write down your goal and put it where you can see it often—on the fridge, on the bathroom mirror, in your daily planner or journal, beside your desk or workstation, or elsewhere. Also, write down each significant insight as you step toward your goal.

3. Gather resources. Start looking for the people, programs, and organizations that can assist you on the journey. The better your resources, the faster you should reach your goal.

4. Acquire information. Educate yourself on the specific addiction you are facing. Studies show that those who are more knowledgeable about their condition do better in treatment. They ask insightful questions and sometimes notice things a doctor might miss. As much as possible, become an expert in the area of your addiction.

5. Identify tasks. Give yourself specific assignments: thought patterns to adopt, actions to perform, emotions to express, habits to form, and so forth. Break your tasks into manageable portions and take them one by one.

6. Evaluate progress. Review your progress at defined intervals. Are you making headway? If not, why not? Put your evaluation in writing for future reference, and make any necessary adjustments to your plan.

7. Explore preferences. Tailor your plan and tasks to your individual preferences. You will likely have many choices on your journey: counselors, programs, classes, and organizations.

8. Remain flexible. Don't cast your plan in stone. It exists to serve your growth. If your plan is not getting results over a reasonable period of time, rethink it and make changes. And even when your plan is working, stay alert to ways you can improve it.

9. Pray continually. When you pray, you're not talking to the wall or to yourself. You are talking to God, and he hears you and responds. Prayer is a genuine and powerful ally on your journey. It's not your prayers that have the power; it's God on the other end of the line who has the power to do what you cannot do. Don't take one step without talking to God about it.

10. Pace yourself. This is a journey, not a race. Few changes happen overnight, no matter how hard you work or pray. Give God time to work, and be thankful for the little changes you see.

We are pleased that you are so interested in following God's way to freedom from your addiction. We pray that the God in whom we live, move, and exist will guide and sustain you on the journey, both today and forever. God bless you!

—Henry Cloud, Ph.D.
—John Townsend, Ph.D.
Los Angeles, California

Prayer is

a genuine and

powerful ally

on your journey.

๑

Embark on a
Life-Changing Journey
of Personal and Spiritual Growth

DR. HENRY CLOUD

DR. JOHN TOWNSEND

Dr. Henry Cloud and Dr. John Townsend have been bringing hope and healing to millions for over two decades. They have helped people everywhere discover solutions to life's most difficult personal and relational challenges. Their material provides solid, practical answers and offers guidance in the areas of *parenting, singles issues, personal growth,* and *leadership.*

Bring either Dr. Cloud or Dr. Townsend to your church or organization. They are available for:

- Seminars on a wide variety of topics
- Training for small group leaders
- Conferences
- Educational events
- Consulting with your organization

Other opportunities to experience Dr. Cloud and Dr. Townsend:

- Ultimate Leadership workshops—held in Southern California throughout the year
- Small group curriculum
- Seminars via Satellite
- Solutions Audio Club—Solutions is a weekly recorded presentation

For other resources, and for dates of seminars and workshops
by Dr. Cloud and Dr. Townsend, visit:
www.cloudtownsend.com

For other information **Call (800) 676-HOPE (4673)**

Or write to:
Cloud-Townsend Resources
3176 Pullman Street, Suite 105
Costa Mesa, CA